Somewhen

GILBERT LUIS R. CENTINA III

Published in the United States by:
CreateSpace, an Amazon.com company.
First Edition
New York, New York

Library of Congress Cataloging-in-Publication Data
Recommended entry:
Centina, Gilbert Luis
Somewhen
p. cm.
Summary: Looks at man's relationship with his Creator's abiding love and mercy despite his constant failings.

ISBN-13: 978-1483956626
ISBN-10: 1483956628

1. Centina, Gilbert Luis 2. Poetry Book-Religious 3. Poetry-Asian-American General 4. Biography 5. Title
PN 6099 2013

7 9 10 8

Manufactured in the United States of America

DEDICATION

To Francis of the Poor,
First Roman Pontiff from the Americas

CONTENTS

CONTENTS

CONTENTS

ACKNOWLEDGEMENTS

Grateful acknowledgement is made to my parents
for inspiring me to write again and for their unconditional love
and support; to the Augustinian Recollect community of St.
Nicholas of Tolentine Monastery at Union City, New Jersey,
U.S.A. for their hospitality; to the devotees of St. Charbel,
especially Saba Massoud; and to Benny Igwebe and the faithful
of Holy Rosary Church for their abiding faith.

LETTER TO MY PARENTS

I left home to seek
The path to the heavenly
City, where the sun

Never sets, where lights
Converge into a stairway
Of solid sunbeams

Leading to the choir
Conversion, font of our faith
That never wavers

I will not look back.
Your love will always help me
Stay on higher ground.

UNSENT EMAIL TO POPE FRANCIS

In humility
the Church gathers together
The flock you shepherd.

In simplicity
the Church becomes his people
Him alone to serve

Through you he reveals
The mystery of his love
Embraced by his Church.

AURELIUS AUGUSTINUS

From sinner to saint,
You played peekaboo with God
To seek earthly forms.

Systole of grief,
Diastole of anguish
Filled your mind and heart.

Then the Word of God
Rectified your straying soul
With its fire of love.

Inflamed by this love,
You soared straight toward the Truth,
Following the light.

FOR JOSÉ MORÁN FERNÁNDEZ

Who wants to be spared
From the enigmatic sphinx
Must cross the unknown

From the ocean deep
Ghosts of sharks spawn piranhas
To control rivers

For peace and order
Sharpened razor teeth showing
To dispense their greed

Vision of vultures
Feeding on bloodied corpses
Of the innocent

Vision of reptiles
Celebrating their triumph
Like burning candles

Vision of spiders
Grotesquely undermining
The landscape of faith

As the mind paddles
Between the Yes and the No
Truth is jeopardized.

OF THOSE NOT ORDAINED

So when wisdom fails
The system must be restored
To revive the faith.

The Spirit hovers
And the deeply wounded soul
Ceases to resist.

In Cassiciacum
The Word filters the conscience
And lends it courage.

Whispered in cloisters
Truth now speaks the parable
Of those not ordained.

We share their travails
As we salute them. Brave souls.
Indestructible!

YOUR UNFINISHED DREAM

Your unfinished dream tells you
You are not in purgatory;
Your trip to heaven
Is a work in progress
So you are not in hell either.
From where you sit you can see
Someone peering from inside
The pupil of your eye,
So you pinch yourself to reality.
There's no doubt about it.
Your unfinished dream
Happens to be you.

BY THE EAST RIVER

I sit down but never weep
Over the misfortunes
Suffered by the discarded and unloved.
Why should I not rejoice, Lord?
When Zion is just a breath away?
Let me sing your praises, Lord.
You are my boss. You know
How to take good care of me.

ARS POETICA

Once again I am one
With the destitute, the exiled,
The oppressed. Of them I sing,
With them I share
My passion
For the dispossessed,
My burning love
For the underdogs.

DARK FORCES LURK BEHIND ME

Like overly friendly strangers
Furtively plying their deadly wares
To impressionable children.
At times they titillate
The trusting and the gullible
Who mistake love for greed,
The root of subhuman misery.
Sensing their terrible intent,
I keep my faith and pledge
My allegiance to my Creator.

SOJOURN

A hemisphere away
I hit gridlock
And come to a sudden stop
In the corridor
Of human indecisions,
Which make virtue
Of patience stretched to the limit
For those who bear in mind
That good comes to those who wait.
Like the voyagers of yore,
I have always thought that nothing
Changes more than
The faces of the seasons;
I eagerly await
The ocean to cover the earth,
The earth to swallow the ocean,
The ocean and the earth
To bring about
The Armageddon.
But I have discovered none too late
That hopeful waiting is in the end
Its own reward.

TRIP TO HEAVEN

From my unhappy homeland.
The journey leads to heaven,
Compassed by stars and stripes.
Who can divine the wisdom
Of the Inscrutable?
Who can discern the will
Of the Almighty?
Thieves and usurpers,
Propelled by dark angels
Of relativism,
Terrorize my unhappy homeland.
Emboldened
By the people's hopelessness,
They sow havoc and confusion
As they invoke God's name.
They make pact with the Devil
As they suppress dissent.
Life becomes as dispensable
As the price of a single bullet
In my unhappy homeland.

SOMEWHEN

So you want to know
How everything is going?
Nothing much.
Which is to say
Solutions are sealed
In the lips
Of so-called friends, brethren,
Colleagues, comrades-in-arms,
Where I am, first among equals
Is a self-serving slogan.

LORD, ARE YOU STILL THERE?

L ord, are you still there?
Lord, are you that unreachable?
Lord, must you remain forever silent?
Lord, must you hide your face
Away from me forever?
Lord, why are those ordained
To mediate between you
And their fellowmen
Garble your gospel of truth and love
With their pharisaical nonsense?

NETWORKING

When friends call
Or email me
Their joyful acceptance
Of my being where I am now
As part of God's most holy will,
I tell them not even Zeus
Can prevent Destiny
From fulfilling
What must come to pass.
This is no time
For myths and lores.
I am back to Christ's parable
Of the mustard seed.
I urge them to pray with me
That whatever we sow here
In East Harlem may be
According to God's plan
So it may grow and bear fruit
And yield a rich harvest
In the fullness of God's time.

MANHATTAN

A midst the silence
Of the skyscrapers
That at night overwhelm
My humanity
With their gravity,
I know you are
Just around the corner
To hear me unburden myself
Perhaps under the flicker
Of a solar-powered street light
Or at the next stop sign
As I head toward the promenade
Where Manhattan overlooks
The sleepy Hudson river
Glowing faintly
Under the crescent moon
As constant as the wave
Of would-be immigrants
Longing to have a taste
Of the Big Apple.
There is no other way
To express myself
And for you to listen.
When I reach what Madison avenue
Image makers have dubbed
As the center of the universe,
I visualize your face embedded
In the zipper headlines
It is then that I can hear you.

DEO GRATIAS

Today I receive a letter
Which turns out to be
An official order
Issued by my Provincial
Attaching me
To the circumscription of Spain
And assigning me
To Holy Rosary community
In Manhattan.
Deo gratias!

SPANISH HARLEM

In East Harlem
Spanish is the only language
Immigrants care to speak.
When I hear them talk
I remember the first
Augustinian missionaries
Who evangelized my homeland
And taught our forebears
The story of Jesus.

Jesus, it is great to be here
Working in your most holy name,
Among immigrants.

FRIARS

They are gathered here,
Three seekers of truth
Who have found
The highest form
Of chivalry
In the vineyard of the Lord
This part of East Harlem:
Angel, impresario of veladas
Back in our university days
When wasted manpower
Was as alien as terror attacks
And the faithful made
The sign of the cross
In honor of the Blessed Trinity
Every time they met three friars
Walking together
In white habit for the tropics;
He is the soft-spoken angel
Who speaks the best Spanish
This part of East Harlem;
Pepe whose Sephardic blood
Vibrates in his recipes
For our weekend meals
When Yolanda the cook
Takes her weekend break;
The friar who puts work
The main ingredient of his life
This part of East Harlem;
Abel the philosopher,
Whose hospital ministry
Enriches our community life
With cleanliness and godliness.
They labor tirelessly,
Unceasingly, joyfully
In the vineyard of the Lord
This part of East Harlem.

HIS ABSENCE LEAVES A TRAIL

I remember Nicanor
The wunderkind.
He worked like a horse
And labored with dignity.
The silent walls of Holy Rosary
Proclaim his heroism.
He struggled alone
To combat hubris,
Lost countless battles
But ended up winning
The spiritual warfare
By leaving behind
A much better world
Than he found it.
Eloquent was this man.
His life did speak.
His absence leaves a trail...

TO BASILIO ÁLAVA SAÉNZ

L et us follow infinity
In wisdom and in grace.
Let eternity resound
Until the last penny
Is spent on God's kingdom.
The house of God must be rebuilt,
It has been left in ruins for so long.
For that they need a friend:
A friend who can share with them
Life's surprising twists and turns;
A friend who can show them
God's loving providence and care;
A friend who can tenderly and firmly
Lead them to the City of God.
God's people need you.
Stay.

VIGIL

When you see angels
Dancing their way to heaven
Through the eye of a needle,
Reality becomes a playground
Of your childhood dreams.

TO MY BROTHER PIERCE

Today is your birthday
Twenty-first of November
Two thousand and five,
In the year of our Lord,
Feast of the Presentation of Mary.
This is not a birthday poem
To be read in a party
As acquaintances become friends
In a gathering of complete strangers
As neighbors are kept busy
With their crowded lives.
Rather it is a hymn of praise
To our living God,
Also a thank-you gesture
To our parents
For bringing you into this world.
Happy birthday!

FELLOWSHIP

This church remains open.
Christ himself, the good shepherd,
Is the pastor here.
This is God's house.
He is our loving father.
This house is yours and mine,
God has made it to be ours.
His love has gathered us
Together. His love
Has made us his children.
Leave your cares behind.
Welcome.

LATE AT NIGHT

L ate at night, when I burn
The midnight oil
And read on and on until
I can read no more,
Time takes its toll.
Sounds and shadows
Yield to dazzling grace.

JOSÉ HERRERO HIJOSA

You speak of civil war
  That stunted the growth
Of little children.
You were a child
Who lost your toys
Among the rubbles.
In the spring of your life
You endured one arctic cold
To the next, devoid of heat.
You woke up
Shivering under the aegis
Of stentorian pharisaism,
Gothic and frightening
Like a horror story.
You took your religious vows
Only to have your life mangled
By *frailuchos* whose parents
You never had
The chance to know.
Even in summer,
Your martyrdom never ended
In Colombia or in Venezuela.
You were shoved
To the Big Apple
Where one winter,
For a couple of weeks,
You became delirious with fever
When the boiler broke down.
You suffered the inconveniences alone.
The Peruvian priest you temporarily relieved
Had gone to Machu Picchu with some relatives.
At eighty, the pull of autumn is irreversible
And you look weary and sober as truth.
You say it is your duty
To die. You chaff at pious predicates

Who reshuffle the lives of their subjects
Like a deck of cards
On a gaming table.
Now their gilded cages are empty
As the seasons end one more cycle
And finally shut the door on them.
These predators have run out of birds to prey on
As impressionable boy sopranos shun their rooms.
Unlike what came to pass with you one summer
In the spring of your life
At an unguarded moment
When you strayed from your parents' house,
Made a detour and stumbled your way upon
Those foreboding walls
That devoured you
And you never came home.

AT MARYLAKE

Thank you, dear Lady, for calling us
To seek refuge at your sacred shrine.
Together we make our pilgrimage
Here at Marylake, abode of the blessed,
Where wise men, instead of suffering,
Offer to God their trials and pains.
Show us the safest trail to holiness
Far from the clutches of evil snares
Free from polarizing human enterprise.
As we partake of his sacrament of love,
May we find in our earthly cul-de-sac
Peace and comfort from our living God.

MOMENT OF TRUTH

Truth is like the moon.
It waxes and wanes and plays
Possum in the night.

Truth is like the sun,
Covered by bipolar clouds
In the broad daylight.

At the right moment,
Sure as the moon and the sun,
Truth splendidly shines.

RECKONING

They try to smoother
Truth with the palm of their hands
In a cover-up.
Truth fights back and scalds their flesh,
Strikes them dumb and starts to speak.

OFFERTORY

Father, I willingly accept
This cross you give me as a gift.
I take up with all my heart
This cross you give me as a gift.
Treasures count as dust beside
This cross you give me as a gift.
Glory and grandeur pale before
This cross you give me as a gift
Father, I offer back to you
This cross you give me as a gift.

NOONDAY

Where this cordillera ends I do not know.
Up here I must retrieve my username.
The sky is clear and the sun is shining,
Still I cannot find my username.
Swans are gliding on the lake,
Still I cannot find my username.
Trees are changing the color of their leaves,
Still I cannot find my username.
The trail may lead to nowhere but I know,
Up here I must retrieve my username.

WE MUST FORGIVE

Want to see God's image
And likeness in us?
We must forgive.

Want to hear God
When he speaks to us?
We must forgive.

Want to sing
Of God's goodness to us?
We must forgive.

Want to smell
God's presence in us?
We must forgive.

Want to feel
God's love for us?
We must forgive.

COEXISTENCE

Treasonous spiders
Scheme cobwebs of deception
For truant fireflies.

Noisy ducks and geese,
Observing strict boundary,
Sail the lake with swans.

Bees do not whisper
The secrets of the lilies
To their drones and queen.

BEFORE THE STORM

Why can't the blind see?
Vipers have poisoned
The honeycomb.

Why can't the mute speak?
Vipers have poisoned
The honeycomb.

Why can't the deaf hear?
Vipers have poisoned
The honeycomb.

Why can't skunks smell like roses?
Vipers have poisoned
The honeycomb.

Why can't demons love like angels?
Vipers have poisoned
The honeycomb.

APPEAL

Fiery Israfil,
　Hold your trumpet still
Wait till man is ready
To pass through
The eye of a needle

TESTED BY FIRE

Ardent Israfil,
Trumpet muted at his lips
Tested me by fire.

"Not malleable," he said,
"Your heart is no gold.
You alone can program it.

"Not hard as diamond," he said,
"Your heart, like the moon,
Waxes, wanes: full, half, quarter.

"But more than the moon
Your heart is purely human.
You know how to love."

THE HABIT OF DEATH

D eath is a stalker
Relentlessly pursuing
All the world that breathes

Like a skilled hunter,
Hiding with chameleon ease,
Patiently waiting.

Once our time is up
At the twinkling of an eye
Death shows us his face.

TO LIVE WE REHEARSE TO DIE

We need to rehearse
From the moment we wake up
Till we go to sleep.

Morning we get up
To start another journey.
Evening we come back

To lie down on bed
Shaped like a coffin. To live
We rehearse to die.

PARABLE OF THE WICKED

How can we counter
The sting of the brotherhood
Of night? Like shadows

They linger, ready
To strike, lethal as scorpions
In the dark, wily

Spiders that spin
Their network of wickedness.
They flourish like grass.

THE WICKED PROSPER

The wicked prosper
When the just are divided
When the just are scared

Like neutered rabbits
No voice escapes from their throat
And they close their eyes

They refuse to hear
And they strangle their conscience
The wicked prosper

THE JUDAS VIRUS

The Judas virus
Captures the holy temple;
Its keepers are gnomes.

Creatures of the underworld,
Plying their rubrics and runes,
They worship Mammon.

They work to obtain
Wealth and glory and power
By trading their soul.

PROVERB

When we reach the top
There is nothing more to climb
We return to earth

To restart our life.
The very people we meet
On our way up there

We see them again:
This time they are going up,
We are going down.

BECOMING

Do not be afraid
To be what you want to be
To be what you are

To be who you are
To be what you need to be
Do not be afraid

You are what you are
You are what you want to be
Do not be afraid

REQUIEM TO ROMEO RAMOS CENTINA

Farewell, big brother,
Go rejoice in the Spirit!
Ransomed by the blood

Of our Lord Jesus,
Stand now before the Father
To behold his face.

Go join the blessed.
Where time ceases, where the Lord
Eternally reigns.

TO THOSE WHO DO NOT

To those with eyes to see but refuse the light
To conceal their sophistry of cloistered deviltry
And gloat over the slaughter of the innocent,
Protect and nurture the termites that gnaw
At the spiritual fabrics of human symmetry;
To those with ears to hear but do not listen
For fear that dialogues may provoke
Transparency that can unravel
Criminal cover-up of perverse dimensions
Kept in the archives of so-called authorities;
To those with tongue to savor truth
But misuse it instead to fabricate untruths
Who never hesitate to gain a hundredfold,
In exchange for a lifetime of want and misery
Not in the name of God
But in the name of dominion;
To those with nose to smell but avoid
Sniffing out the rat that carries the plague
And feeds on carcasses, drinking vile blood
Of their hit-and-run victims by the wayside
To surrender to the twisted appetite of worms;
To those with the skin to act like beasts,
To change the rules of every game they play
With lesser mortals whose lives they treat
Like a stack of chips in a baccarat,
Waving their joker like a magic wand
In their vainglorious roulette of self-deception.

No!
No!
No!
No!
No!
This is not for them.

GNOMIC YEARS

You ask me why all these gnomic years
I have ignored their assaults on my sacred honor
Like a bluebird locked up in a golden cage
Refusing to announce its loss of freedom;
Or like a mascot tortured by lightning,
Plugging both ears to maintain equilibrium;
Or like a swarm of fireflies in a windy trail
Ambushed by the glares of fake lights;
Or like a lamb stereotyped as a scapegoat
By mercenaries camouflaged as missioners;
Or like a box of scandals wanting to explode
For justice and truth to shine in splendor.
Am I resigned to tomorrow's absurdity?
Not totally. I still can choose my destiny.
Life is not mine to give or mine to take.
How I must live my life depends on me.
All these gnomic years I seek refuge in silence.
Sufferings can consume words and speeches.
When the croaks of frogs prevail over reason,
Larks and nightingales opt not to sing.

LETTER FROM NOWHERE

Pen becomes a stranger to ink
bleeding dry and empty from disuse
like a laptop that has squeezed out the last juice
from its lithium battery pack
its cursor blinking and throbbing
as if gasping for air before sinking
into the black hole of a 17-inch
flat screen monitor as life reaches
a dead end in places like ground zero
where i had inhaled its rarefied air
within what used to be its floor-to-ceiling
glass-encased windows to the world
a must-stop for students of architecture
until some cavemen thought of a way
to topple it from the sky with a weapon
of mass destruction that even the evil geniuses
of wars past could not have concocted
in the wicked alchemy of their minds
that they had rented out for the devil to use
as his workshop conducting lessons on hijacking 101
to fly winged birds of hellfire into
where i used to look down at grids of cars
crawling in traffic one hundred and ten
floors below and marveled at how this creature
crafted by man wrapped in steel skin could make
even a ten-wheeler seem puny like a matchbox
that we keep warning our niece samantha
from making part of her valuable toy collection
sitting down the basement of our sister's home
arranged like items on display for sale at toys "r" us
in anytown usa or at fao schwarz along fifth avenue
by central park where joggers take a minute
to smell the roses and gawk at their reflections
on the pond by the skating rink that donald trump
had saved from the mosses that grew there

as the big apple struggled with its yawning budget gap
while the rich and famous alight from their limousines
across the street in the plaza to enjoy
being seen at the oyster bar
talking incessantly about the latest
this and that at wall street or the blah blah blah
about some big star in hollywood or the yada yada yada
that goes on in their self-absorbed pastime
that no designer stop watch can interrupt
(come to think of it gotham adorns itself
with clocks from battery park
up to where the riverside drive meets the bronx)

so now you wonder what has kept me
from touching base with you for so long
the plain and simple answer is that
nothing upon the transom of my existence
was worth writing home about
but since you have gotten me started
i might as well use the necessary punctuations:

You see, I live among vipers, hissing with lies,
Flummoxed at how these spineless predators
Can self-inflate like helium balloons at a party store
With their shelf life going only as far as the next pin prick.
Do I really care?

Do not return to sender:
There is no way of knowing
Where I am.

ST. CHARBEL

L over of silence,
From the land of Lebanon,
Lofty as cedars.

Reaching for the skies
You chose to follow Jesus
Through self-denial

And simplicity.
In silence you read God's plan
For you to serve him

To pray for the lost
Ones, to bring them back
To God's loving arms.

REMEMBERING

I asked for a sign:
"St. Therese, three red roses!
Please...three red roses!"

Nobody wanted
To discuss my foolishness.
So many doors

Were waiting to be
Opened. A sign was needed
To answer the call.

My girlfriend sent me
Three red roses, duly signed
"The Little Flower."

PRAYER

God of our graces,
You are my boss.
You ransomed me from death
By dying on the cross.
I offer you my nothingness.
Out of nothing
I am nothing, Lord.
Without you I am a broken vessel.
Breathe in me your Spirit, Lord.
Make me whole again.

THEY

With their false piety
    They all lead a double life,
They play politics

Among the brethren
Who are sworn to renounce it.
What does it profit

For them to profess
Their fealty to God? Are they
Not Mammon's servants?

Whited sepulchers,
They are the killers of God:
Blind leading the blind.

KEEP THE FAITH

When God seems asleep
He is very much awake.
He hears every sigh

Of every victim
Of human rights abuses.
He feels the anguish

Of all those detained
Without trial. He collects
Every tear they shed.

He turns them to pearls
Invaluable and priceless.
Keep faith. Hang in there.

WAR WOUND

The war wound my father wears
Is the shibboleth of our tight clan.
It cuts so deep it never heals, no scar
Can hide the hurt he suffers,
The apotheosis
Of a World War II veteran.

MY FIRST POEM

My first poem I dedicated to you.
(You have no equal, you are the best,
My number one mentor, the irreplaceable cook,
The indispensable presence, the morale booster,
Pillar of strength, heart of our happy home,
Geyser of flowing similes and metaphors,
You are the first word I learned to master.)
When a girl cousin published that poem as her own,
The only line she skipped I now write to you:
Mother, I love you!

Made in the USA
Charleston, SC
30 May 2014